Let's Get Down to
BUSINESS

Let's Get Down to BUSINESS

LESSONS FROM A SERIAL ENTREPRENEUR

RAYSHION SASHINGTON, MBA, MBC

WESTBOW
PRESS®
A DIVISION OF THOMAS NELSON
& ZONDERVAN

Copyright © 2017 Rayshion Sashington, MBA, MBC.

All rights reserved. No part of this book may be used or reproduced by any means, graphic, electronic, or mechanical, including photocopying, recording, taping or by any information storage retrieval system without the written permission of the author except in the case of brief quotations embodied in critical articles and reviews.

WestBow Press books may be ordered through booksellers or by contacting:

WestBow Press
A Division of Thomas Nelson & Zondervan
1663 Liberty Drive
Bloomington, IN 47403
www.westbowpress.com
1 (866) 928-1240

Because of the dynamic nature of the Internet, any web addresses or links contained in this book may have changed since publication and may no longer be valid. The views expressed in this work are solely those of the author and do not necessarily reflect the views of the publisher, and the publisher hereby disclaims any responsibility for them.

Any people depicted in stock imagery provided by Thinkstock are models, and such images are being used for illustrative purposes only. Certain stock imagery © Thinkstock.

Scripture taken from the King James Version of the Bible.

This book is a work of non-fiction. Unless otherwise noted, the author and the publisher make no explicit guarantees as to the accuracy of the information contained in this book and in some cases, names of people and places have been altered to protect their privacy.

ISBN: 978-1-5127-8873-0 (sc)
ISBN: 978-1-5127-8872-3 (hc)
ISBN: 978-1-5127-8874-7 (e)

Library of Congress Control Number: 2017907872

Print information available on the last page.

WestBow Press rev. date: 6/7/2017

I dedicate this book to my parents, J. D. and Jestine Sashington, for pouring into me and helping me to realize my dreams, and to my wife, Niki, and daughter, Raelin, for believing in me and not allowing me to quit.

CONTENTS

Acknowledgments ix
Preface xiii
Introduction xv
Chapter 1 A Born Entrepreneur 1
Chapter 2 Do You Have a Business, or Is It a Hustle? 11
Chapter 3 Get Up, and Get It Done 21
Chapter 4 You Don't Have to Be Perfect 33
Chapter 5 Discipline and Accountability 45
Chapter 6 Ask the Right Question—Now 55
Chapter 7 Business Has to Work for You 65
Chapter 8 Use Someone Else's Money 75
Chapter 9 Start the Way You Want to Finish 85

ACKNOWLEDGMENTS

I would like to first thank my Lord and Savior, Jesus Christ for all that He has done and I know through Him all things are possible. I am reluctant to single people out, but I would be remised to not acknowledge my Siblings and Family, closest friends, spiritual leaders, teachers and professors who poured into me, my Sash team, my fraternity brothers, friends, and mentors who helped me accomplish my goals. Life is a journey and somewhere along that journey we've had the opportunity for our paths to cross and for that I am forever thankful. I am grateful for the support and knowledge that you have bestowed upon me and may God continue to bless you and your loved ones.

Commitment means staying loyal to what you said you were going to do long after the mood you said it in has left you.
—UNKNOWN

And all things, whatsoever ye shall ask in prayer, believing, ye shall receive.
—MATTHEW 21:22 (KJV)

PREFACE

I grew up in the Englewood neighborhood of Chicago. It's now one of the inner city's most dangerous areas, but growing up, I made it my personal land of opportunity. My dad owned a waste management company, so I had the good fortune to grow up around a business from a very young age. It was a window into the world outside our neighborhood, which was filled with people of all races and ethnicities. It broadened my view of what was possible. I never felt like I was stuck; I always knew I would be successful. I also knew from a very young age that I wanted to be a businessman.

Some people are born with the gift to create music. Others can build the most beautiful furniture from a few pieces of wood. There are mechanics who can literally fix anything with a motor and engineers who bring to life robots, electronics, and spaceships. I was born to establish and run businesses. I have a knack for it. I understand not just how business works but how money works.

I started my first business when I was eleven years old, which provided leaf and snow removal—two seasonal commodities Chicago had an abundance of. I identified a target market and pursued potential customers vigorously. As the business grew, my friends asked if they could help out, and I gave them a small percentage of the money I earned. But I did not share equally. I kept the majority of the money because I was getting the contracts and taking all the risk. And it was my reputation on the line. I didn't know it at the time, but I was already a businessman and an entrepreneur.

Fast-forward a couple of decades, a few college degrees, and many successful businesses later. I've come to believe it's not enough to simply do well. You need to also help others do well. That has become my purpose: to share all the corporate, academic, and hands-on, real-world knowledge I've accrued with people who also crave to be business owners. People who dream of starting their own companies are people who have an entrepreneurial passion and drive for business. Through this book, I can reach out to and connect with anyone eager to learn the tips and strategies I have developed and utilized over the years.

This is not a shortcut. Starting and running a business is hard work that requires total commitment. This book is designed to give you the foundation you need to start building your own success story, one that not only benefits you and your family but your community and beyond.

INTRODUCTION

I am a serial entrepreneur. From the time I was eleven to now, I have invested in, owned, or had direct involvement with multiple businesses. During that time, I have accrued valuable experience and knowledge in how to start a company and how to create a business. And make no mistake; while they are opposite sides of the same entrepreneurial coin, starting a company is not the same as creating a business. Each activity utilizes different skill sets.

The definition of *a* business is simple: an enterprise that provides goods and/or services to consumers. But *business* is more complex. It's what enables you to reach your goals and achieve success. Business makes things happen. Understanding business is necessary to pursue your passion, fulfill your purpose, and make your business (company) a success.

My purpose is to help others achieve their full potentials. So I've written this book to share some key points on how to take an idea and turn it into a thriving enterprise. The business strategies and tips I present here—use someone else's money whenever possible, understanding good debt, fear is a good thing, don't expect perfection, being accountable to your word, the importance of personal discipline, there is no dumb question, and understanding what works for you today, and start the way you want to finish—can help you build a sustainable business. They are lessons I learned personally or from seeing others, like my dad, struggle through trial and error

Building a business isn't magic. It is a skill, and skills can be taught and learned. Every entrepreneur faces unique challenges because no two businesses are the same. Just like no two people are the same. Everyone has their own unique sets of experiences, perceptions, goals, visions, and circumstances. But there are some basic principles of business that are the same for everyone. This book is designed for the nine-to-five employee who has an idea and dreams of starting his or her own company. It's also for the struggling small-business owner who is spinning his or her wheels because of ineffective systems or business practices in place. The information presented is intended to give you the foundation for success by explaining fundamental strategies and how to implement those strategies in real-world situations.

So let's get down to business.

CHAPTER 1

A Born Entrepreneur

By education, I am an accountant. By nature, I am a businessman and venture capitalist. If you name some type of business, I've probably invested in it, managed it, or owned it—no matter if it was a beauty shop, clothing store, grocery store, or gym.

There is no denying formal education is important for many business endeavors. Diplomas and professional degrees still carry a lot of weight to most employers and to some clients. Not only do they show you have a certain expertise, those pieces of paper also symbolize dedication, responsibility, and a sense of purpose. However, education can only take you so far because nothing is more important than hands-on experience. Diplomas may look pretty on the wall, but they aren't going to keep the doors open if you aren't willing to put in the time and effort to be a successful entrepreneur.

Although I was blessed with the opportunity to attend college, it is not my academic background that will help *you* get down to business. It is the lessons I have learned as a serial entrepreneur over the years. I'm not talking financial theory here; I'm sharing real strategies and offering proven tips I've learned in the start-up trenches, starting as a kid, watching my dad.

I knew at a very young age that I wanted to be a businessman. There was nothing I wanted more, so I soaked up everything I saw. I realized early that at the core of any successful business is a strong work ethic, which my parents instilled in me. They raised me to believe you can have anything in the world you want if you're willing to work for it.

Another early lesson was you must set your mind to it. People will always have reasons why you shouldn't take the risk, so you have to find the fire and passion within yourself. With me, it was always there, even as a kid, raking leaves or shoveling snow, and as a college grad, working my first job. I would always tell myself my career wouldn't start until I owned my own business. Everything else was just a job.

My dad came from a different place. His move from employee to entrepreneur was prompted by necessity. He was the smartest man at the waste management company he was working for, but when it downsized, his bosses let him go. They moved on without him.

So he decided, "I know everything I need to know; I just need to get the capital to get started." He got a loan from his brother for five hundred dollars and came up with another five hundred dollars on his own. So with that thousand dollars, my father went out, found a truck, and established his own business. He got clients the hard way: by going door to door. At that time in Chicago, waste management was controlled by a few large companies. There were no small waste management options. But everybody loves to deal with small business. And my dad's motto reflected why: "We're large enough to serve you, but we're small enough to know you."

That right there, just seeing him build his business one client at a time, gave me my first sales experience. Then working in his office gave me accounting experience. As I got older, I interacted with so many people and types of businesses—it might be a clothing store, it might be a restaurant, it might be a bar or a lounge, or it might be a Laundromat. I was able to interact and know the inner workings of so many different businesses.

I also learned every situation is a valuable learning experience. Even if you're an employee at a company you dislike and dream of owning your own business, you should try to learn everything you can while you're there. Make every day count. Be present in the moment because everything you learn you'll apply to your own business later. It's a different kind of education, but it can be the best kind of education.

I say all the time, "The best education I ever received I paid for with my time as an employee." I held myself to a higher standard. I always believed, "Okay, I have to put my best foot forward, no matter what I'm doing or how I'm doing it." As soon as I finished graduate school, I went to work at Wachovia Bank, and it was one of those situations where I soon started to hit the ceiling.

During the job interview, everybody said, "Oh, you're going to have so many opportunities for career advancement." So after working there a while, I applied for a position that I was qualified to fill. But when it was time to discuss the salary for the position, they didn't want to pay the listed salary, claiming it would be too much of an increase.

While working at the bank, I started one of my businesses, so I was building that on the side during my free time. Once my managers learned about my business, it was quickly frowned on. Their position was that it could become a conflict of interest, yet they were unwilling to pay me the listed salary amount for the position I had applied for. For me, that was the last straw. I had a choice to make; I could stay or move on. I decided to bet on myself. So the first thing I did was pay off everything I owed except for my house and my student loans. My only bills were my mortgage and a student loan payment of $140 a month. Once I did that, I left the bank.

It wasn't as scary a decision as it might be for others

because I already had experience running my own business. In college, I did an internship with an accounting firm. The executives liked everything about me and offered me a position to do tax accounting. After doing that for a year, they asked me, "Now do you want to buy a franchise?" So while I was still working toward my MBA, I bought my first tax office.

Let me just say that balancing graduate school and running a business at the same time took all my time. Fortunately, I was very young, didn't have a lot of responsibilities, and didn't need a lot of sleep. I remember those days vividly. I was just determined, and that's really what it comes down to. I saw something in front of me and decided I had to take full advantage of the opportunity. It was like I was walking around with blinders on. I would go from school to the bank to the business. There wasn't a lot of playtime.

Honestly, though, the biggest surprise was how much money I earned in my start-up by the second year. That was why it was easy for me to walk away from my job. I always had the notion that, in the worst-case scenario, I could always find another job. Knowing that enabled me to focus 100 percent on growing my business. I worked to establish the first office clientele of individual and small business clients. Within two years, I opened a second location, and from there, I continued growing the business.

It's funny, but growing the business was the easy part; the hardest part was learning to let go and hiring people. I learned

I'm just one person and cannot do it all. But the business was my baby, so I hovered over all of it. This was financially unhealthy and stunted my entrepreneurial growth.

As hard as it was hard to let people in, it was harder to find the *right* people to let in. The hiring process was complete trial and error. I would receive a résumé and think, *All right, this person looks great on paper.* But when he or she came in, it was not so great. I had to learn to identify the right people for my organization. I determined that people with an entrepreneurial spirit and committed to great customer service were ideal. I needed people who wanted to grow with the company.

There is an obvious irony here. If you find people who have that entrepreneurial spirit, odds are there will come a time when they will want to run their own businesses. But as funny as it sounds, that's okay. It's not just about me and *my* business. I have always wanted to help people, and what better way to help people than teaching them how to help themselves? Of course, not every person wants to be an accountant or own a tax-services business. However, I believe across the board, regardless of the industry, you will find business practices that are similar within any successful company. Everything from establishing a culture devoted to customer service or to the simplest truth that you can't spend more than you earn and expect to succeed.

That last truth took me a while to grasp. Growing up, my family was one of the youngest on our block; most of our neighbors were elderly. That's what gave me the idea to rake leaves and shovel snow. There was a need, so I created a business to fill that need. I made good money. And spent it all. I had to learn the value of saving. My mom taught me a different value. If a customer paid more than my going rate or gave me a tip, she'd say, "Oh, no. Go give that back." She didn't believe in overcharging or getting more than what you agreed to. Later, I learned the importance of charging what you said you would charge, even if something takes longer than expected. In the end, honesty and integrity will win you loyal customers who keep coming back and recommend you or your service to others.

As I got older, I sometimes helped my father out on the waste trucks to earn extra money. I preferred that over working at McDonald's. I was never really into working at fast-food restaurants. I worked at one fast-food place for maybe two or three months when I was gathering money for my prom, and I hated it. For me, it was either working with my dad at the waste management company or finding something different.

I think part of my work ethic came from having five siblings—three older brothers, an older sister, and a younger sister. We have a large family, so I grew up wanting to do my own thing my own way. I didn't want to follow in anyone else's footsteps. I wanted to earn my own money, so I could buy whatever clothes or shoes I liked. I took no interest in waiting for someone to do it for me.

As I got older, I started reflecting on the traits that came as second nature to me. I started to discover and understand my gift; the thing God put me here to do. For me, it is to teach others what I know. I realized I shouldn't take for granted the things that come naturally to me. It is a blessing. And it was time for me to share all I knew instinctively and all I've learned over the years to help others.

This awareness happened around 2007, the time of the financial crisis. That's when it really clicked for me, and I started thinking about how I could help others. It was then that I started a nonprofit called the S.A.S.H. Foundation, which is an acronym for Stand and Save Humanity. I started this foundation to help people become financially independent. I wanted to bridge the gap between financial independence and improving the socioeconomic status of people who wanted to change their ways of life.

I wanted to do something different. I knew that money alone wasn't enough to make me happy. Now, don't get me wrong. Having money is fun and necessary, but it's not what drives me. I don't wake up every day thinking, *Money, money, money*. When the economy crashed, I saw so many people who were in disarray, wondering, *Where do we go from here?* They were lost.

So I started doing a lot of consulting work. I often found myself giving my clients advice they didn't always want to hear. I would tell them straight out that they might have to switch careers or start a different business. And, of course, I helped them do just that. I helped them learn how to run a business. It became less about the accounting formulas and more about the actual how to run a business—processes and systems, financial strategies, how to track inventory, plus the intangibles. All of which I now share with you.

CHAPTER 2

Do You Have a Business, or Is It a Hustle?

The purpose of this book is to share some key business points. One of the most important is also one of the most basic: do you have a business or do you have a hustle? A hustle can be defined as selling or promoting energetically and aggressively. When I think about a hustle, I think of someone waking up every day with no set goal in mind except to just make some money for that day.

You can do honest, legitimate work, but that doesn't mean you have a business. I love my father; he was my role model and showed me everything about being in business—eventually. But to be honest, for a long time my dad only had a hustle. That didn't change until after I returned from college and applied what I learned in school. Only then did my father's waste management company become a true business.

This is something that is always in the back of my mind. So often I'll hear people say, "Yeah, I'm in business." Then they tell me all these things they are doing, and I sit there thinking, *You're really not in business; you're just hustling.*

Understand, there's nothing wrong with hustling, but if your company or start-up is only a hustle, you're limiting yourself. Having a business drives you to want to be goal-oriented, with the enthusiasm to grow your company, not just to make money. Implementing processes and strategies to grow your company is when you formulate your business. In my professional relationships dealing with banks, clients, investors, and potential investors, I came to understand what it really takes to be in business as opposed to having a hustle.

Let me give you an example. I have a friend who cuts grass. It's usually just him, but he has someone to help him occasionally. He defines himself as a sole proprietor, but that doesn't mean he has a lawn-care business in comparison to someone who also started by cutting grass and landscaping, but they also developed a marketing plan that secured more customers, hired employees, implemented a payroll system, purchased more equipment, offers insurance, and leases an office. So while my friend is still doing all the work himself, this other entrepreneur has not touched a blower or a rake in years. He concentrates solely on growing the business.

Yes, both bring in money. But my friend hasn't moved ahead because he is busy maintaining a hustle.

I saw both sides with my dad's company. When he first started out, it was a definite hustle because he was doing it all by himself. For him, starting his waste management company was not the pursuit of a dream. It was a necessity; it was how he would feed his family. But after ten years, he started to understand he could have a business. That's when we took the steps to get him incorporated. Once it was a corporation, he could create a tax structure, expand, and become sustainable. He even made it possible to pass the business along to a second generation (me). If he had just kept hustling, it would have been him handing me the keys to the waste truck and saying, "Okay, here. You can go do this now." You can pass a business from one generation to the next, but it's hard to pass a hustle along to someone.

Turning a hustle into a business requires practical planning and personal commitment. You also need to have a vision of what you want, whether it's simply to be the best waste management company in your town or to be a driving force nationally in your industry. You also need patience. Building a business is a process that requires time and effort, so patience is an important business virtue.

Branding is also important. You must start building the business with the brand in mind. For example, the brand of my father's business was built around customer service and community involvement. I remember one client he worked with all the time, and they organized in the community to help people get medical care at a local clinic.

When I got my first franchise, my brand was all about professionalism and client appreciation by offering the best product at the best price. And like my father, community involvement has always been a thing for me. My nonprofit the S.A.S.H. Foundation creates this outlet for me. I believe strongly in giving back. You can't just take away from a community; you have to deposit something good into the community.

A business, unlike a hustle, requires planning. A business plan is a good place to start this process. What is your goal for this week? What's your goal for one year? What's your two-year plan? Your five-year plan? It helps to write down a plan because once it's on paper, you are accountable to the plan and the brand.

Planning lends itself perfectly to being organized. Whether you use a tablet, a smartphone, or old-school notebook and pen, keep track of what you need to do. Concentrate on the most important items first and then work your way to the least important task of the day. A helpful tip is to group similar tasks together. While multitasking can be a good thing, it can also cause things to fall through the cracks, so better to do two things really well than four things poorly. Building a business is a process, so take it one day at a time, and you will get there.

One of the most notable differences between a hustle and

a business is the ability to hire employees. It's not enough to just have people who work for you. It is important to hire people who will work as a team to help your business grow to its full potential. The culture of teamwork begins at the top with you and the environment you establish. Bosses who rule through intimidation will never get the best from their employees. You want your staff to have pride in themselves and the work they do for your company. And don't forget: a little encouragement and appreciation go a long way.

Now, having employees and a successful business doesn't mean you get to kick back and take it easy. You are the person responsible for the livelihood of your employees. So you have to go out and create the jobs every day. That is the business of it. Whether it's for two people or two hundred, you need to constantly have work for the people you employ.

Turning a hustle into a business doesn't mean you are home free. It is just the beginning. Be careful to continue putting in the time and energy to grow your business because you can slide back into the hustle. I've seen it happen. A prime example is a general contractor I knew during the big housing boon back in the early 2000s.

He had set the business up the correct way, creating the structure and everything of that nature. He may have had as many as twenty employees and was able to secure multiple jobs that supported everyone. But he started spending too much money on personal things, leaving his business without any cushion.

In any business—and I mean *any* business—you're going to have a downturn. There are peaks and valleys in everything. So when those valleys came for this man's business, he wasn't prepared. Taking money out of the business for extravagances made it impossible to keep the legitimate business solvent and moving forward when the downturn came. As the economy started to unfold a little bit, he was only able to secure jobs he could do personally, so he had to let all his employees go. He might hire a temporary helper if the job called for it, but mostly he was back on his own. Hustling.

Using your business bank account to pay your personal bills is a danger for a lot of new businesses. Over time, many entrepreneurs tend to mingle their business and personal finances. That's just what start-ups do. At first, it's for necessities, like paying rent. Then later the vacation to Cancun suddenly comes out of the business rather than personal savings account.

Occasionally it's used as a tax strategy. Some small business owners hate paying taxes and use their company as a personal checking account to support their lifestyles. Those lifestyle expenses can hurt the value of your business. At some point, you have to set up a financial structure to prevent this from happening. Also, it's important to pay yourself a salary and pay your taxes. Be careful to not use the business's earnings as personal disposable income, which is a common practice when you have a hustle.

You must understand that earnings are not necessarily

profits. Just because a business brings in $250,000 doesn't mean you have $250,000 to play with. The business itself has expenses and then you have expenses. If business expenses are $100,000, and your personal expenses are $100,000, there is $50,000 that is pure profit. Some entrepreneurs find it hard at times to have a 401(k) plan and other savings plans. But if you implement sound business practices and grow the business, then that *is* your retirement. When the time comes and I say, "Okay, I'm ready to sell. I'm done with this. I'm ready to retire or do something else. I can get the tax accountants to come in and value what my business is worth and negotiate a sales price." And now, guess what? I'm retired.

The problem with a hustle is no one is going to buy a hustle. You cannot retire on a hustle.

That is one of the many things I learned from watching my dad. I would say I learned about 70 percent of my business knowledge from being around my dad and the other business owners he interacted with. The other 30 percent came from the classroom and running my own businesses. I remember when I was still an undergrad, one of my guidance counselors looked at my résumé and asked, "Why are you here?"

It was funny to me and strange to hear this question from somebody who is supposed to help you achieve your academic goals in higher education. But she looked at what I'd already done and said, "Most people aren't going to do half of this when they finish here. You've already done more than half of it."

However, the reality was that degree still mattered. I told her, "Unfortunately, society dictates that I need this piece of paper to keep growing, so …"

I was lucky because I had the best of both worlds. I was able to see the inner workings of a business growing up. I was also able to go to school and get the degrees that provided some opportunities I might not have otherwise received. In college, I realized that even at a young age, I had a God-given instinct for business.

When I started my leaf removal and snow-shoveling business as a kid, it clearly started out as a hustle to get a little bit of money here and there for sneakers, candy, and whatever else. But as time went on, I realized I could make more money if I marketed the right way. I understood supply and demand for my business. I lived in a neighborhood where most people were older. That was my target market. Then I came up with my target price, and from there, I started thinking like a businessman. I grew the business, and it went on for quite some time.

An important part of supply and demand is evaluating price, product, or services offered. You must determine if an adjustment is necessary. In my childhood business, eventually the dynamics began to change. There were competitors undercutting my prices, so I had to ask myself if I was going to lower my prices to compete or if it was time for me to move on to something else. For me, it was time to move on to something else.

Do you want a hustle, or do you want a business? The answer depends on your goals and dedication. While there's no shame in having a hustle, you have to understand that no one is going to put time, energy, or money behind a hustle because it only takes care of one individual. It is much easier to find people who are willing to put time, energy, and money behind a business because it can benefit many individuals as well as communities. Do you want a hustle or a business? Making this decision very early on allows you the time to do the work, and put the systems and strategies in place to get there.

You know, in the United States of America, business creates synergy, or brings together businesses. This synergy in business produces tax dollars, jobs, and the revenue we need in this country, in our states, and in our communities. This helps to keep all of us going.

Again, there's nothing wrong with having a hustle. But if you want a business, you must start working on the business of being in business. You have to be proactive. It won't just happen on its own.

CHAPTER 3
Get Up, and Get It Done

Just do it. Refuse to lose. Don't hope for it; work for it. Get your game on.

Sports are full of slogans that all basically mean the same thing: Get up, and get it done. That might seem like such an obvious tip that I should just stop now and move on to the next chapter. But for many people, taking that first step is the hardest part of being an entrepreneur.

On the surface, it's so simple: start moving. But procrastination is our built-in emotional default mode, so you'll always be able to come up with rational reasons to wait. "I just need to get more organized." "I want to have a little more in my savings." "Maybe I should begin after the holidays." It's surprising how many of us talk ourselves completely out of doing something. We'll find every reason not to do it versus finding every reason to do it.

The bottom line is this: You must decide if not now, when?

People pride themselves on having this great idea for a business or some terrific product that's going to be the next Swiffer or GoPro. You can talk the talk all day; it won't mean a thing if you don't walk the walk. Realistically, you will never be an entrepreneur if you don't get up and do it.

One person I really like listening to is Joel Osteen. He once quoted Les Brown, a well-known motivational speaker. He asked where the richest place on earth is.

> This place of endless riches is not in the Middle East, where there's rich, black gold buried deep beneath the Earth's surface. Nor is this place in South Africa where there is a plethora of diamond mines. The wealthiest place in the world is a cemetery. Now you may ask: *For what justifiable reason is the wealthiest place in the world a cemetery?*
>
> Simply put, in a cemetery you'll find that there are books that were never written. There are songs that were never sung. There are ideas that were never acted upon; dreams that were long forgotten. If one were to die today, then what ideas and what aspirations would die with him or her?

I think of those words every time someone tells me about his or her great idea rather than about how the person is pursuing that great idea. In that cemetery, there are so many businesses that were never started. So many products never developed. So many successes never achieved, movies that have never been produced, books that have never been written, and inventions that were never designed—all because people didn't do this one thing: start.

Do like the Nike swoosh, and just do it! Put one foot in front of the other, and get going. Even if you don't know exactly what direction to go, just move.

The older I get the more aware I am of our tendency to always live this life as if tomorrow is always promised to us. Even though we don't like to dwell on it, we all know that is the furthest thing from the truth. Tomorrow is not promised to any person. We should always be watching the clock. So if you want to make that life-altering change for yourself, for your family, for your legacy, or for whatever, you have to get moving.

Let me get a little more specific for those who aren't sure exactly how to start getting down to business. First, we must get out of our own ways. So often I see people overthinking it or even talking themselves out of it. *What if it fails? What if it doesn't work?* Listen, it often comes down to taking that step of faith and saying, "Okay, let's get it done."

We can sit around on the couch and talk about it: "This is my step 1, this is my step 2. I got step 5, but I don't know steps

3 and 4." You have to put one foot in front of the other and go. In life, there's no road map that says, "This is exactly the way you go." As you start a business and start to progress, you can't predict what will happen. The market itself determines which way you'll need to shift to grow the business, and you have to be flexible and able to shift on the fly. But to even get to that point, you must start the business in the first place.

I understand that the biggest part of not moving is fear. When you talk about business, there are a lot of unknowns. "I got bills that I have to pay, but I don't know where this paycheck is necessarily going to come from." That's the whole gamble of betting on yourself. It's different from being an employee where you say, "I'm going to dress up and fix my résumé the right way, so I can go get this job." Being in business, I have to fix my résumé every day, I have to put this suit on every day, and I have to show up every day to keep the business going. Some people don't want to work that hard, while others are afraid to.

The way I see it, fear is a good thing. I went to a conference where they talked about how fear is not meant to stop you. It is meant to wake you up. What are you so fearful of? When you walk out your door to face whatever you're facing that day, you should have no fear.

Growing up in Chicago's South Side, I carried fear every day of my young life. I was a shy child because I was fearful of where I might end up and choices I might make. My father used to tell me, "For every one good thing that you can find out here, there are ten bad things, and you have to know how to recognize them." That was his way of telling me I had decisions to make, and just because doing something makes money doesn't mean it's a good thing to do. There are a whole lot of ways to make money on the South Side, but that doesn't mean they are good things to do; and certainly, they weren't all legal. So I had to choose. Am I going to be a good person who does good things to make good money? Or am I going to be a person who is just dedicated to making money?

My fear was basic. I had a lot of friends doing a lot of things. I had friends driving very nice cars at sixteen or seventeen years old. Hmm. But if you take that path, where can you really go, what can you really do going forward? So as a kid, I started to understand the longevity of life. We spend a lot of our youth wanting things you're not supposed to have at nineteen years old because most teenagers don't know how to handle it and don't think past that day. I've always wanted to keep whatever I acquired for the long term. That comes from seeing my father live within his means. So many friends I grew up with live above their means and then fall by the wayside. When you apply those lessons to business, the lesson is that just because you see it doesn't mean you must have it. I promised myself as I got older that I would not live my life that way.

I had to decide not to be fearful. You should do the same. Don't fear; God has you. He will never let you fall too far. Trust fear is here to wake you up. It's here to get you up, and get it done. Whatever your idea is, you have to make it tangible. Whatever your invention is, you have to get it in production. Whatever it is that keeps you awake at night because you can't stop thinking about it—that goal, that passion, that purpose, that calling—is there for a reason. Are you going to answer it?

And here's the thing. The longer you wait, the harder it's going to be to get moving. I think the older we get, the more set we are in our ways. A lot of it comes down to becoming comfortable in a certain lifestyle. We become attached to a regular paycheck, even though that paycheck and that lifestyle might not be the best things for us because we're not stretching ourselves. You might have this burning thing in you that says, *There's more out there for me. But am I so attached to this paycheck and this lifestyle that I'm not willing to gamble on myself to go get it done?* And the fear of the unknown will keep you doing what you already know.

I know how people think. Their paychecks could be only $200 a week, but they know if they show up that week, they're going to get $200, no matter what. While there's a 50–50 chance they could make $2,000 next week, there's also a 50–50 chance they could make nothing. So that guaranteed $200 seems a lot more stable. You just have to get out of your way. You have to step up, and you have to try.

This doesn't mean you can't go about it in a methodical way. Before I left the bank to run my accounting franchise, I stayed long enough at my job to pay off all my bills except for my mortgage and student loans. I wanted to have as little debt as possible. That was part of my plan. And a plan is always a great thing because when you put it down on paper, it becomes a general guide—even though I've always been told that if you want to make God laugh, tell him what you're going to do. However, I find when you prioritize things, put them down on paper, and arrange them in order, what you need to do will become that much clearer.

I am fascinated at the number of people who are working to start a business with no plan of any kind. A part of getting up and getting it done is to have a well-thought-out idea of what needs to happen to get you from point A to point B. For many people, debt is a barrier. When I first started, my biggest concern about leaving my job was that I needed to have health insurance.

I was very young, but I was already thinking along the lines of, *Hey, when I leave here, I'm not going to have health insurance.* I started shopping around for a plan, and an agent came into my office. Ironically, it cost me less to get health insurance on my own than the premiums I was paying working at the bank. When I first started buying my own health insurance, it was $120 a month. At the bank, I was paying $300 a paycheck. And I got paid twice a month. Apparently, I had to help pay for all those unhealthy people I was working with.

To my point, I had to get up, quit my job, and go do it. At some point, you have to totally commit to your business and take a leap without the safety net of that weekly paycheck, or in my case, a group health plan. What we see as a safety net gives us a false sense of security. And really, in this day and age, is there any security? I don't know anyone who has been in the same job for more than a decade. It just doesn't happen.

My parents' generation routinely worked at one job for thirty-plus years. When they retired, they got a good pension they could live comfortably on. Those days—and that kind of security—are gone. I have a thirty-year mortgage, but I'm not guaranteed a job for more than a year, much less thirty years. And if you are unwilling to bet on yourself, I don't know who's going to bet on you.

Once you get up, you need some sort of direction. Remember, a plan is just a general guide that you will constantly adjust as situations change. I started with a five-year plan, but the business grew so quickly that I had to readjust it after two years. Early success didn't mean I could sit back and relax. You must always keep moving, and you always have to make sure to get out of your own way. To this day—right now—I am working to get out of my own way, get it done, and leave it in God's hands. His grace is what's going to lead you sometimes.

And don't worry about anyone other than yourself. One of the worse things you can do is compare yourself to what other people are doing or worry that they have more success than you. I encounter this often with people I counsel.

Someone will come in and say, "I want to start a business because I see Jane Doe or John Smith doing very well at it, and they live the lifestyle I want."

First, you cannot do anything based on what someone else is doing. People do things for different reasons. Everyone has a unique set of needs, goals, passions, and purposes. A lot of times, people pursue a business out of necessity—like my dad did. He put his blood, sweat, and tears into getting his business off the ground because its success meant feeding his family and keeping a roof over our heads. Necessity is a completely different impetus than simply the desire to have a business that enables the part-time entrepreneur to take a better vacation or indulge in a hobby.

Those two scenarios come from very different places internally. If you are pursuing a business as a hobby, you're likely not giving it your all. It is highly unlikely you'll achieve the same level of success and accomplishment as a person who has given it his or her all. So trust me when I tell you there is never a comparison to what someone else is doing; everyone must run their own races. The blessings God has for one person are different from the unique blessings He has for you. Live within your own faith and in your own purpose. You cannot live through another person's purpose.

You also cannot be deterred by negative people. Sometimes to move forward you have to ignore the naysayers, so they don't get in your way. Naysayers are not going to tell you, "Oh, you should do that because you will do well at it." No, they are going to say, "You shouldn't do that because it will never work. There are too many just like it. What do you know about running a business?" They will plant seeds of fear. If you listen and think about it long enough, you'll find a hundred reasons why you shouldn't do it.

Don't. Take that leap of faith and say, "This is what's preordained for me to do." Stop listening to the naysayers, or you'll never get anything done. They—whoever "they" are—hinder us from doing what we're supposed to be doing.

Every person in life has a calling. Sometimes you have to get to that quiet place in your life and listen carefully to hear and understand what your calling is. Everyone's calling will be different. Everyone's life will be different. Every person's experience and level of success will be different, and we will all live different lives. Don't compare your life to others. That isn't your life. You must get up and get moving on *your* path.

Life is a journey! Are you up for the journey? As you set out, cast aside the dream snatchers who are lurking, waiting to shoot you down.

"Man, that's not going to work."

"Why are you doing that?"

"Why are you trying to do this?"

God put the dream in you, and you're responsible for chasing it. Confidence must come from within. If you don't believe in the business or products, how can you expect anyone else to believe in it. You have to be your biggest cheerleader. But selling your dream requires action on your part. Get up, and get it done!

The Bible says, "Faith without works is dead." James 2:14-26 NKJV So we can have all the faith in the world, but if we're not willing to do the work, it doesn't matter. What are you waiting on? We have to move, and we have to keep moving. There is no excuse that is good enough. When I made the decision to join a fraternity, there was a poem I learned that always stuck with me.

> Excuses, excuses are the tools of the incompetent.
> They build monuments of nothing.
> Those who specialize in them seldom accomplish anything.

If you're walking, breathing, moving around, there is no excuse. If God woke you up this morning, you have no excuse. Nothing is holding you back but you.

CHAPTER 4
You Don't Have to Be Perfect

Nature seems full of perfection—the perfect sunset, a perfect snowflake, or even the perfect spring day. Unfortunately, people and businesses can only ever strive for perfection. It's a journey, not a destination. As the poet Robert Browning wrote,

> Ah, but a man's reach should exceed his grasp,
> Or what's a heaven for?

Meaning, to achieve anything worthwhile, you should attempt even those things that may seem impossible.

I don't know of any business anywhere that is perfect. I don't care how much money it makes, how many people are employed there, or how much good it does for its community or the world. There is no such thing as a perfect business. So why put the added pressure on yourself to achieve perfection? The important thing is to start and get the business going; you can fix things as you go along.

I'm not sure where this push for perfection came from or when exactly it started. When my dad was starting his business, he knew if he simply did the best he could, things would work out. "Do your best" was always the encouragement given to me, not "You have to be perfect." That's the furthest thing from the truth. I think in this era of big data, we think we can analyze everything down to an exact science, checking forecasts to determine the perfect time to jump in the market.

"Right now is not perfect because of my family situation." "It's not perfect because I don't want to lose my health insurance." Perfect is the one thing you don't have to be. In life there's always going to be something. There is no perfect time to jump in the market. There is no perfect time to leave a job. There's not even a perfect opportunity.

But that doesn't mean it isn't the right time to jump into the market or the right time to leave your job or the right opportunity. The important thing to know is that there will always be challenges to meet, there will always be obstacles to overcome, and there will always be a storm on the horizon. You will have highs, and you will have lows; the key is how you handle the adversities as well as the successes.

It's also important to know your strengths and weaknesses. Nobody is good at everything. Nor do you have to be. If you already have employees, delegate. If you are just starting out and need help, outsource by finding help using online staffing sites. There is no point in looking for perfection in everything that you do, and you don't even need to be a jack of all trades. Find what you're great at, and rock with it! The things you aren't so good at outsource.

I know I'm great at some things and not so great at other things. The things I'm great at I capitalize on, but I don't waste my time on things I'm not great at. I find someone to outsource the task to and move on.

For some reason, many people think others expect them to be perfect, especially in work situations. Those are the folks who, when asked in a job interview what their weaknesses are, are compelled to say, "I'm good at everything!" No one is good at everything. Nobody is perfect. And there is no perfect company.

What a prospective employer is looking for are honesty and self-awareness because being in business will humble you at times. It teaches you to practice a lot of humility. So knowing what you're good at and what you need to delegate or outsource is crucial whether you're an employee or an entrepreneur with a start-up.

You cannot make it in business believing you're perfect or believing you know it all. If you go into business thinking you're the greatest, you'll be completely unprepared to deal with things when adversity strikes. To succeed, you need to adopt a different perspective. You need to be humble. You need to take time to sit in silence and reflect on your purpose. Be at peace with imperfection. Make it an affirmation: "I'm not perfect, this company is not perfect, and that's okay. I'm not setting out to be perfect. I'm setting out to start and grow this business to where it's supposed to be."

Too many people spend so much time trying to figure out the perfect time, the perfect opportunity, the perfect place, the perfect organization. I learned early that the pursuit of the perfect anything is futile. I'm a calculated thinker and know I'm prone to overanalyze. So I just had to tell myself, *Sometimes you just have to get moving.* Put one foot in front of the other and get going. I realized that if you wait to be perfect, you'll probably never start. So before life passes you by, get off the porch, and pursue your purpose and passion.

You can't micromanage your life. It's kind of like having kids. On one hand, for most people, there's really no perfect time to have children. There's always a reason to wait a little longer—until you have more money, more time, more patience, a bigger house, a more secure business. But when they come, you make it work. You adjust, you adapt. It's the same with business, especially if you have another job, and you're thinking about being an entrepreneur. If you wait for the perfect moment, you'll suddenly find yourself retiring without ever having tried.

Just because we know intellectually that no business can be perfect, that we can't be perfect, it is easy to get stressed out over it. Most entrepreneurs are perfectionists—and driven—so you have to develop coping mechanisms to balance that part of your nature with the realities of business. I now have a workout regimen I follow every morning. I get up between 5:30 and 6:30 in the morning and work out first thing for an hour before starting my day, which helps me focus. Then as the day goes on, with the inevitable bumps and bruises, ups and downs, having that mental clarity enables me to say to myself during a challenge or during a time of transition, *It's okay. I can handle this.*

There are all kinds of obstacles with business beyond the economy, market conditions, and net sales. You have to deal with vendors, competition, employees (whether staff or outsourced), and with customers; especially customers. Not every customer is going to think you did a perfect job. Sometimes customers are going to be unhappy about one thing or another. How you handle that kind of adversity defines your business more than any success you may achieve.

If you maintain an attitude that you are perfect, things are not going to end well when dealing with unhappy customers. You will most likely lose the customer and harm the reputation of your business because people talk. One happy customer may tell one person about his or her experience, but one unhappy customer will tell twenty people about the experience with your business. And thanks to social media, customers can reach even more people. Yes, there are some customers who will never be happy. We all encounter those individuals at some point. But even then, you must at least listen and consider their complaints. Learning to handle adversity effectively means admitting you, your business, and business transactions in general are not perfect. Mistakes happen. Miscommunication happens.

What should never happen is going back on your word. I think the most important lesson I learned from watching my dad was to always, always do what you say you are going to do. Do not make expedient promises you have no intention of following through on. That is a kiss of death to a business, especially a start-up. In those times of customer dissatisfaction your character is developed by following up and following through to try and solve the problem.

Another thing I learned is that when a person is upset, you simply cannot take it personally. It's a business complaint, not a character assassination. Even if they are upset, it doesn't necessarily mean that they are upset with you. Sometimes you just need to let people talk. They often simply want someone to listen; they want to be heard. Don't interrupt, don't give them advice; just let them say what they need to say and then come back to it.

Say a customer calls with a complaint. If you let him or her talk for two or three minutes without interrupting, most times that will completely change the tone of the call. You have taken the time to show interest and to really hear what is bothering the customer. Almost always, the person will then say to me, "Well, I wasn't really mad at you, but I'm just kind of upset because ..."

And once you understand the reason, you can then say, "Let's talk about how I can help you." But if someone's really, truly upset, and you try to talk over him or her, you will not get anywhere because you're not listening in that conversation. There will be no resolution, and you will likely lose a customer.

Before you can help, you have to listen. Whatever you say you're going to do, you have to do. When you think about it, your character is made in those moments. I like to take ownership of things. So in those moments, there's an opportunity to step up and be the bigger person. Here's a prime example. I worked at a CarMax when I was in college. One day a customer came in who had purchased a car. She was irate because the car wasn't working properly. Customer service and other employees kept passing her around. I worked in the business office, so I was probably the last person she needed to talk to, but there I was, on the phone with her.

Understand, in the customer's mind, it's one company. He or she doesn't care about what you do or what department you work in. If you are the person the customer gets, he or she is right; it should not matter. What people expect to see most of the time is for whoever answers the phone to take ownership of the problem.

So instead of passing her on to the next person, I told her,

"Let me do this. I'm going to give you my name, my number, and this is the department that I work in. I'm going to go and connect with the people who need to get this resolved for you, and I'm going to call you back."

So that's what I did. I talked to someone in our service department. I talked to the sales manager and even talked to the business office manager. From there we could figure out the problem and resolve it for the customer. As a result of that situation, I was promoted because I took care of the problem without handing it off to someone else, even though technically it wasn't my department. The lesson there is if you want to be a leader, you have to step up and lead. And remember, it's your character on the line.

I look for the same kind of leadership in my employees. As I said before, I'm all about value and customer service. So when I see someone handle a problem, even if it's out of his or her official job title, that shows me the leadership within that person.

When I'm looking for someone to spearhead a special project or when I am opening a new location or looking for owner-operators, I remember the person who showed leadership abilities. I'll think, *Okay, that person might be good for this position because of character and leadership skills—two things you cannot teach.* Everything else—processes, accounting methods, inventory, ordering, and all those nuts and bolts of a business—can be taught. People often debate whether leaders are born or developed, but in my experience, some people instinctively take ownership of a situation or problem. Those are people who strive to be the best without trying to be perfect. The bottom line is, if you can't take ownership of a customer or client's problem calmly and thoughtfully, your business is probably not going to sustain itself.

The flip side is also true. Let's imagine you are unhappy with one of your vendors. Maybe a delivery was late or a product or service wasn't up to your standards. I find that if you go in honestly and say, "Okay, we have a problem. I'm not angry at you, but this is what happened," you have a much better chance of getting a satisfactory outcome with that approach. If you start the conversation angry and yelling, quite frankly, you give them a reason not to help you. If you make it personal, you run the risk of alienating your vendor.

Now there are times when it may be necessary to stop doing business with someone. There is a difference between not being perfect and negligence. You have to have standards, and if someone consistently fails to meet those standards, it's time to move on. That is a part of business also. Every business relationship will not be beneficial, much less perfect. So don't be afraid to find something different and then just move on.

In business, you will handle more than just obstacles or negative problems. You also have to adjust with success and growth. How you start out today will likely change considerably five years from now—or even just five months from now. You have to be able to pivot when the market or your business needs to make a turn. The ability to identify and navigate those adjustments is the difference between a missed opportunity and a sustainable business.

When I speak about clarity of mind, I don't mean compartmentalizing. Years ago I went to Steve Harvey's Act Like a Success workshop. Mr. Harvey created the program to help people reach their full personal and professional potentials. His mission statement was simple but powerful.

> I firmly believe that each and every one of us is born with a gift. A gift that allows you to live a life of joy, peace and prosperity. The challenge that we all face, is to identify that gift, learn how to cultivate that gift, and then use that gift to create personal success.
>
> As an entertainer, businessman, father, husband and friend, I have learned so many lessons along this journey. Lessons that have taught me the dos and don'ts of setting powerful goals—and reaching them. Lessons that have come to me—not just from my successes, but also from my failures—that have allowed me to build my businesses, develop loving relationships, experience financial success, and to keep setting bigger goals.

It was a very impactful workshop. When the instructor, Lisa Nichols, talked about the four quadrants of success, it really stuck with me, so I wrote it down. I look at that list every day.

The first is the spirituality of success, having some spirituality within yourself and working on that and toward that. The second part is relationships: your family, your friends, your love, and your colleagues. The third aspect is finances and the business itself. The final quadrant is health and wellness.

Every day I take out that list, read it. And then ask myself, "Am I working on each one of these every single day?" You need to have them all to reach true success. I can have all the finances and businesses in the world, but if I'm lacking spirituality or a relationship with my family, friends, and colleagues, am I successful? Is it worth having all the money in the world if my health and wellness are lacking, and I can't enjoy life?

Take Steve Jobs. He had what seemed to be an endless well of money compared to most people, but he couldn't stop his health from declining. Those four quadrants of success are what I've learned to work within. Like Steve Harvey says, "Act like a success. Think like a success. Be a success."

Steve Harvey is an example of someone who found his purpose and passion and used them to become even more successful while helping others. He started as a stand-up comic and went through some hard times. He developed a personal philosophy on how to be successful, which brought him more fame and financial security. He wrote books and started workshops to share his insight with others. Like Joel Osteen, he inspires people to reach their full potentials. People like them inspire me to pursue my purpose to help others and inspire them to follow their passions.

But before you can achieve success, you must take that first step. Resist the urge to weigh yourself down with unrealistic expectations of perfection.

CHAPTER 5
Discipline and Accountability

Some people are born with the "discipline gene." They have innate restraint and willpower. For others—myself included—it is a learned behavior. Often after a hard lesson learned. I was just a kid when I was offered my first franchise. I assumed I was disciplined. I had gone to college, did my schoolwork, and earned degrees. I got up every morning and went to my office, where I ran a business and met with clients.

I was making really good money. I was also spending it. One of the first lessons I learned was just because you make the money, doesn't mean it is all your money. There is something about seeing your bank account grow. It's like handing a twenty-something kid keys to the new car and telling him or her, "Hey, you sit in it, you can listen to the radio, but you can't drive the car yet." The hardest thing to understand was how to properly manage the money as it came in. For me, the money came so fast that I assumed there was an endless supply.

I was finance major in college, so you'd think I would be prepared. But it was trial and error for me, too. And to be 100 percent honest, in my first couple of years, I probably made a million dollars. I also spent a million dollars.

I relate it to being an athlete. Today's professional athletes sign huge deals, mostly when they're young, and they think, *Okay, yeah, I'm going to make all this money forever.* What they need to understand is no, you're not. You're going to make this money for this short time, so you have to manage it and make it work for you. For example, many rookies in the NBA make around $800,000 a year. They see a check with that many zeroes and immediately go out and buy a flashy car or go out to the clubs, footing the bill for their friends. They don't consider that they have to pay taxes on that money and pay their agent and/or manager. So they may only have $350,000 to spend.

It can be really easy to get behind. Trust me, I know. In some ways, I'm still making up for my wild spending when I was younger because that's money I could have been investing in my future. Now I won't lie; I had a whole lot of fun while I was spending that money. But when you finally wake up from the high of having the money, there is an, "Oh, no, what did I do?" moment.

When I was very young, I met a personal banker who told me, "Look, no matter how much you make, live as if you're only making half that amount. So if you make $100,000 a year, live as if you only make $50,000. Then, if there is an unexpected expense, you can afford to pay for it. If you lose your job, you'll have money to live on while you secure new employment. If you start a business, you have a cushion for any slow period or money to invest and expand your business."

One way to manage your money is by creating a budget for your business and for your personal spending. I stay within a budget in my personal life as well as in my professional life because one can't supersede the other. My personal life can't have a huge budget and my professional life a small one because that will leave me robbing Peter to pay Paul.

Having discipline in the beginning is very important. This helps to lay the foundation for your business, and we all know that if you have a strong foundation, you can easily build upon it. Whether you start as a sole proprietor or as a corporation, you have to start by creating a realistic budget based on your salary and stick to it. This will assist in maintaining accountability that sets you on a path toward becoming fully sustainable.

When you start to pay yourself a salary, you have the opportunity to invest the rest of the company profits into growing or strengthening the company. If you don't create a budget or a salary for yourself, you could overspend, which could be fatal to your business.

The challenge of money management requires discipline.

As an entrepreneur, it is difficult to have a lot of savings because you're looking to keep growing. And every entrepreneur knows the old saying is true: "It takes money to make money." When you become disciplined, you can build your credit and financials, eventually working your way up to using someone else's money (e.g., a bank loan or venture capital). When you get to that point, you're able to start saving some real money.

Now there's more than one way to save. You can put money in the bank, but I prefer asset management as my savings strategy. Meaning, my company *is* my savings. For example, let's say I have a business and pay rent for the office space. I eventually look to buy the space, so that becomes an asset for the company. More important, it is an asset that will grow in value. Despite the housing industry problems that we've witnessed, there is only so much land and space for buildings. Also, if you carry a mortgage, the interest on the loan is deductible. So for me, asset management is the way to go.

The flip side of discipline is accountability. Discipline means keeping yourself in line; accountability refers to your dealings with others, including vendors, customers, and employees. Especially employees; that's what I focus on. If you have someone who works for you anytime during the year, that makes the individual an employee. You are accountable to all employees for as long as they work for your company. You can't make selfish decisions that impact everyone around you. For example, if you see something that you want to buy for your personal use, such as a vacation or some other indulgence, and use the company credit card to buy it, that's not being accountable—or disciplined. Accountability in most instances means you have to be a responsible person.

Until your company is established, the only thing you'll have in the business world is your word. So you have to be accountable to your word. Your relationships with vendors, employees, and customers will be largely based on whether you do what you agreed to do. I cannot stress how important this is. If you agree to do something, do it. Don't make a promise you cannot or will not keep.

Another part of accountability is transparency. To be a good leader, your employees should always have a clear understanding of your vision for the company. Expecting anyone to follow blindly is asking a lot. Transparency also provides context and clarity, so employees have a better understanding of their roles. They will also feel more invested in the company's success.

I remember the first time I had to man up and be accountable. I'm a car fanatic. I just love cars, period. I wanted to go out and buy a luxury car. So I convinced myself that it was okay to be selfish. I said to myself, "Okay, I can buy this car and keep the business going and growing." But deep down, I knew buying that car would in some way separate me from my goals. I had to take a step back and say, "I have to be accountable to my company and to my employees. For me to be accountable to my employees, I must be accountable to my vendors, my investors, and whoever else is in the company."

I had to learn that at a very, very young age, but it is still often a challenge. You're young; you see something you really want. It often seems, especially when we're young, that we rationalize we can make it up somehow. We think business is going to go on without change forever, but that's unlikely. The market and economy is always changing. During the recession that started in 2008, a lot of businesses went under. In some cases, it was circumstances, but some entrepreneurs were overextended and unprepared. The lesson is you never know what catastrophe is around the corner.

I got through the recession by having the discipline to make adjustments. In addition to my tax practice, I started selling investments, like mutual funds, to my clients. I added that service because most investors need financial advisers. My idea was to be both my clients' tax adviser and financial adviser. I was always interested in investing—the stock market and other options—even when I was still in school and working at the bank. Like I said, I like learning how money works. Money and investments go hand in hand.

When the economy started to collapse, I realized I had to decide what I needed to focus on and what I needed to let go of. I had to look at my situation objectively. I knew my bread and butter was the tax business. If you look at the big dogs like Wells Fargo and Bank of America, they weren't making any money with investments at the time. So how would I, as a smaller company, compete? So I thought, *Okay, the financial advising right now has to go.* I made the adjustment and focused on the tax practice. I eliminated the investment services side of my business, with the option of coming back to it later.

Currently, I'm looking to offer investment advising as an add-on service again. In 2008 the rules changed, so I haven't jumped back into it just yet. I can't just hang up a sign and start. The new rules dictate that someone else will hold my license, and I will work through that person. The market changes often, as do rules and regulations, so you are constantly learning and adjusting.

In my efforts to be accountable, I made the right decisions before the crash of 2008. I managed to keep all my key employees, which was great. Having to let people go is hard on a company. Finding ways to keep them during a rough patch gives them the confidence to stick with you. I have some employees right now that have been with me over ten years, which would not be the case had I not learned discipline and the importance of being accountable.

When I advise clients who want to start a new business or expand a current company, I always stress the importance of accountability and discipline. Now, on the one hand, no two people are the same, and I advise everyone differently to address their specific needs, wants, and circumstances. I always start out by saying, "Tell me about what you're doing, what you're trying to achieve, and what you want to do."

That's how I learn a little more about them. Some people come in and say, "I want to establish a national chain." Others say, "I just want to do something I enjoy and think I can be good at it."

There is no right or wrong answers. This interview helps me understand what they hope to achieve. The bigger their dreams, the more structure you need to help them create it. And the more discipline they need to be to reach their goals. That's the kind of advice that people need to hear. There is no point in wasting people's time by pretending it will be easy or that they can work just forty hours a week and have weekends off. If they don't know the importance of discipline and accountability, they are going to fail.

I find that people who become entrepreneurs more out of necessity rather than as a second job or hobby tend to be more disciplined and accountable. While necessity may be the mother of invention, need instills determination. My father needed his waste management business to succeed in order to take care of his family. If it had failed, we could have been homeless and hungry.

In my experience, the more mature the client, the more likely he or she is to succeed. I know maturity has nothing to do with age; I've met a lot of very immature older people. But it is also true that many younger people can lack the necessary maturity to appreciate the need to go after the dream now. A younger person is more apt to have the attitude, "I'm going to be here forever so I have time." But as you mature, you start to see things in a different light. The attitude is more, "I have to do this now; I have to get it done today!"

It also takes a certain maturity level to say, "I know where I am right now, but I also know where I want to be five years from now." That shows awareness it won't happen overnight and that there is work and discipline involved to accomplish a goal.

What I want from those I provide consulting services to is to be accountable to me as their business coach. It is vital that we stay on task. Here is a prime example. There was a person I was trying to help, but I finally had to tell the person, "I can't coach you anymore because every time we meet, you go back to square one, and we should be at square seven." It was impossible to get anything done that way, so I said, "I'm wasting your time, and you're wasting my time."

Here is the bottom line. When you start a business, all you have is your word and your work ethic. So be where you say you're going to be, and do what you say you're going to do.

We all want a better life and a better lifestyle. But you cannot grow a successful, sustainable company without discipline. Realistically, if your business is in a growth pattern, purchasing that Bentley or Rolls Royce this year is simply not a good idea. You have to be ready for growth. And if you have all your assets and money tied up in materialistic things, you cannot be properly prepared for growth.

I'm not saying you won't ever be able to splurge. But you have to be disciplined, accountable, and ready when your opportunity to grow comes. Being disciplined means you may have to make sacrifices in the short term for the long-term betterment of your company. It may not feel good now, but guess what? The larger the risk, the larger the return. The sacrifices you make today will result in a big future payoff. You have to ask yourself, "Am I in this for now, or am I in this for the long term?"

Here's a scenario I always throw at people. Today I can make a quick $20,000, but that's all I'm going to make. Or I can take the long route and eventually make $200,000 for the rest of my life. That's the difference discipline makes. You get into business to grow a company and create better opportunities for yourself, your family, and hopefully even the generations after you. If you want to pass on a legacy, you have to think long term. I am unaware of any business that will impact generations without discipline and accountability.

CHAPTER 6

Ask the Right Question—Now

You don't have to have all of the answers. It is okay not to know everything. But it is not okay to not ask questions. This is not the time to let ego, embarrassment, or shyness get in the way of running your business.

Sometimes I think it can be a generational thing. Take my dad. He worked in the industry, so he knew the nuts and bolts of waste management. He had never owned a business, and at times, he made it harder on himself by not asking questions—or not asking them early enough. He went through a continual learning process. Sometimes he would say, "I got this," and then realize he didn't have it. His friends who were also in trucking had the same mind-set. Dad finally reached the point where he realized, "You know what? I'm going and growing, so maybe it's time to get someone else involved."

When we are unfamiliar with something, it can be hard to admit it or even ask for help. Many people would rather fly by the seat of their pants. And while there is value in hands-on learning, it is also important to learn from others. Even though I studied finance in college, I still talked to bankers. I also got a financial adviser involved because I knew with my limited scope I was only able to focus on what I knew. I needed somebody who was unbiased and honest about what we could accomplish.

My knack for finance helped me get to a certain point, but eventually, I started to tread on unfamiliar ground—like managing more money than I had ever seen. I had questions, so I brought in a financial adviser.

This is true for most things in business. For example, if you don't understand the language in a contract, it is okay to say so and ask for help from someone who does. This is important: Never let anyone rush you into a deal. If someone doesn't have time to wait on you to have your attorney or someone else review it, it is not the deal for you.

Likewise, anyone who criticizes you for asking a question may not be the best person to do business with. You must be wary of such people because as you grow your business, you are also building lasting relationships. Anyone rushing you into a bad deal is not looking for a lasting relationship. They want a quick score and are willing to burn bridges in order to get it.

You should have an opportunity to ask any questions you have. There is no dumb question. I cannot drive that home enough. This is your business, this is your baby, and this is what you are trying to grow. You have to be comfortable asking questions.

I've been around business my entire life, so there are things that come second nature to me. I understand what "points" are on a mortgage. I understand what it means to buy down a loan. I don't assume that everyone understands the lingo, and that is perfectly fine. Remember, the one thing you don't have to be is perfect. There are a lot of things I don't know about business, and that is okay, too. The one thing you will never accuse me of doing is not asking the right question. If I don't understand something, I am going to ask. My ego goes out the window. You can never be afraid to ask the question.

I find it beneficial to write down the questions I have. Once you put it on paper, you become accountable to it. Once you're accountable to it, you are more likely to do it. I keep a business journal to jot down any business question that comes to my mind. It's a habit I started about eight years ago because I had so many thoughts about things I wanted to do, and so many things I wanted to find out more about. If I didn't write them down, I surely would forget. Now that the questions are in my journal, I can go back and review them whenever I want. It keeps me from losing my thought process and helps with the focus I need to get things done. In addition to my journal, I keep flip charts and a dry-erase board in my office.

Asking the right question is equally important as learning to listening to the answer. Listening is an underrated learned skill. Ask the question, be quiet, and wait for the answer. There is no point in asking the question if you don't wait for the answer. If everyone is talking at the same time, no one is listening.

Ironically, the reverse is true, too. You need to be receptive when someone asks you a question, especially people who work for you. Be proactive, and let them know you are always available to explain things. Tell them, "I want you to ask questions about things you don't understand. It doesn't matter how basic you think it may be."

The two things I had questions about were how to grow my company and when it is time to stop using my own money. Learning how to use other people's money to grow was vital. When you use your cash reserves, it ties up your available capital. I saw this often with my father. He would always utilize his own capital for new equipment and other purchases, and it left him without cash on hand.

Asking the right questions pertains to more than just business operations. It is also how you find the right people. For example, when looking for a financial adviser, I always start by asking about his or her background as a part of my due diligence. The person I chose had no experience as an entrepreneur, but he had experience working in multiple industries related to finance. His varied work experience was what I was looking for.

One person may not have every answer, but I chose someone who could advise me based on his overall experience. If the person's vision connects with my vision, we can create a partnership. This is my plan with banks now. I tell them, "I'm not looking for a bank anymore; I'm looking for a partner." As I continue growing my company, I need a bank that is willing to take a chance and grow with me.

See, I was a person who always thought bigger was better. I would look at the larger nationwide banks and think, *If I get with them, they can help me go national; they can help me grow my business as large as I want to grow it.* It turns out this isn't always true. I learned that it was easier for me to get deals done with smaller banks rather than with larger banks. For one thing, at a smaller bank, there are fewer people involved in the decision-making. You are more likely to get a response more quickly.

A big bank has to go through several channels, departments, this vice president, and that manager. Then it goes to their analyst, who sends it back through all those same channels. Back in the day, banking was all about local relationships and the community. Although it is different with the bigger banks, it's still about building a relationship. Personally, I found this to be easier with smaller lenders.

Overall, I think start-ups tend to get more traction working with a smaller bank. Also, you may find that there is a greater comfort level with banks. The more comfortable you feel, the more likely you are to ask questions. This helps to create a more personal relationship with your business partner, which in this case is the bank.

Asking questions is important across the board, from interviewing to fill positions to bringing on a new vendor. You don't want to hire the first applicant or sign a contract with the first vendor who comes along. You have to ask the right questions and begin building the relationship. Adopting this mind-set in every element of your business will prove beneficial in improving how you conduct business.

If your cash flow is tight, don't be afraid to call and ask for a payment extension. If you are unhappy with someone's service, call and ask how you can work together to find something that is a better fit for your needs. If you are late on a loan payment, pick up the phone and ask, "Hey, is there any way you could place this payment on the back end of the loan? Or ask if they'll give you a month off and then continue your payment schedule. Most times, they will be willing to work with you. Resist the urge to ignore the issue or never ask for the help. This will just create more problems.

I make it a point to address issues right away. If I dwell on the issue, it can end up hindering a business relationship and keeping it from reaching its maximum potential because I'm the type of person who overanalyzes things. When that happens, it means I'm not thinking about new things or new ideas because I'm still stuck on old points.

There was a incident that made me realize I really need to do this more often. In the early days of me owning a franchise, instead of me just asking where my advertising dollars were going and how my franchise fees were used, I became fixated on those questions. The doubt festered within me, and as time went on, I became upset because I felt nobody was being accountable to me.

Finally, six or seven years in, I started asking questions. And, of course, the response was something like, "What? Why are you asking that question now?" They were suddenly paranoid that I didn't trust them because I took so long to ask. We all should have been transparent from the start.

People grow accustomed to a certain dynamic, and it helps to establish an open dialogue right at the start. I waited six years to ask questions, and it made them wonder, *What have I done to make them not trust me?* When you wait to ask questions after the relationship has been established, it can make people feel they are being accused of something, and the relationship can suffer.

I told them it wasn't about trust; it was about taking an accountability check. I just wanted us to sit down and talk about it. But at that point, they felt offended that I had to ask, "Where is the money I'm paying you, and where is it being spent?" The lesson I learned was that all I had to do early on was ask, "Hey, is there any way possible that from time to time—every few months or annually—we can sit down and have a conversation about how fees are being dispersed and how they're being utilized, and assess if that's advantageous for me and my company?"

Entrepreneurs don't think about scenarios like this when they are getting started. They are so focused on just getting the business going, they don't think of these little details that are the key to building a company with strong relationships. So make asking questions a part of your leadership style from the beginning. Once you make it a habit, it will become second nature.

One of the things that used to drive me crazy with my dad was when his customers paid late. We didn't know when they would pay. He wouldn't ask them about it, and he wouldn't even charge them a late fee. He would always say, "It's okay. It's okay. A slow pay is better than a no pay." I didn't see it that way. How could we effectively manage our business, manage paying our vendors, and employees if customers are paying late, and we're not asking them why? There was no incentive to pay on time because there was no consequence or fee for late payments.

When some clients paid late, it gave me the opportunity to learn about trading goods or services for goods or services, commonly known as bartering. Bartering often benefits both parties. It's becoming a lost art, which is too bad because it tends to be a win-win. I used to barter with some of my dad's clients. If the customer owned a clothing or shoe store, I would go in and say, "Your bill is this amount, and I need some new sneakers. So how about you letting me have these new sneakers, and I'll write it off on your bill." I was happy, the client was happy, and the business relationship was as strong as ever because I asked the right question.

CHAPTER 7
Business Has to Work for You

I tell my clients the business they want to start has to work for them. It has to make sense for their personality, interests, needs, and goals. For example, if someone is an early riser who prefers solitude and loves being outdoors, owning a bar may not be the best match. You may be better suited as a travel guide. Likewise, if you have a young family with kids and a spouse who already works long hours away from home, starting a business that will keep you away from home sixteen hours a day is probably not going to be the best thing for you. A home-based business will more likely suit your needs and give you the best chance for success.

Let's say you want to sell a local product, but you aren't a people person; that business may not work for you. I'm not going to open a nail salon or clothing boutique if I don't want to deal with people face-to-face.

There are some people who are not well-suited to be entrepreneurs. Becoming an entrepreneur means being flexible, going with the flow, and doing what each day calls for. Every day is a little different as you build a business. There are always challenges and unexpected problems to resolve. Entrepreneurship is not for the faint of heart or for those who prefer a stable, steady life.

If you need to get up every day with a good idea of how your day is going to go, if you want to be at work at nine o'clock and off at five o'clock, if you like consistency, owning your own business may not be the best path for your personality.

Business is unpredictable, especially when you're just starting. Sometimes you need to be at work—whether in your home office or a leased office space—at seven o'clock in the morning. You may not finish that day's work until nine o'clock at night. Sometimes you may have to work through the night. I remember my dad worked on his trucks all through the night, come home, get two hours of sleep, and go right back to work. I don't know of any new business owner who has ever been able to have a forty-hour workweek. Oh, it's five o'clock. I'm out of here! When you're the owner, you leave when the work is done.

Now, on the other hand, being an entrepreneur provides flexibility. I've known people who start working at five in the morning and finish mid- to late afternoon. There are also night owls, who don't start working until later in the day and work until past midnight. They are making the business work for them. Obviously, while not all businesses lend themselves to personalized hours, many do.

It's not enough just to have a good idea. You've got to have the right personality for the idea so the business works for you. Otherwise, you will either burn out or grow to hate your business. Either way, it won't succeed. Be honest, and determine if you really want to start a business. Or are you just enamored with the idea of having a business. Ask yourself if you imagine it is an easy way to make money or if you simply fantasize about what being your own boss would be like—without taking into consideration the work and sacrifice that goes into owning your own business.

Then there are those who simply want to be the person full of ideas. They have what they think is a great idea but wanting someone else to start and build the business. "Hey, let's start a business where we repair small engines." But they know nothing about mechanics and don't like getting dirty. People full of ideas really want others to do all the work. They just want to collects the profits. Maybe later, if your company grows and diversifies, you can run the company from afar, but that rarely works for a start-up. The whole point of starting your own business is to have it work for you based on your purpose and passion. So you can build something that helps you meet your goals in life and provides personal fulfillment.

What you also need to know is that just because a business works for you today, it might not in the future. When I was offered my first franchise as an eager young man, I remember looking at that contract in front of me and thinking, *This is my deal. I'm a franchise owner at twenty-something years old! I've reached the mecca of business. Yes!* The contract was for ten years, which when you're in your twenties, seems like a long time. In the business world, it's really nothing.

At that time, the contract—and the business it represented—worked for me, but time passed. I grew older and matured. I started to understand who I was developing into, what my calling in life was, and what God wanted me to do. So when I looked at that contract again after many years, I knew the terms of that contract no longer worked for me. I knew it was time to make a change.

The ability to pivot in business is important because there is no set time when you need to adjust your expectations. Just because it worked for you today may not hold true for tomorrow. The business climate is constantly changing. It might be a matter of months, or it could be years. But sooner or later, your industry will dictate the need for change. We also change as people, so what is good at twenty-five may not be good at forty-five.

Making adjustments ties directly into finding your purpose. If you're just pursuing something because you think it is the best moneymaker, that is not the key to a successful business. Having the passion to do the work to make it a good moneymaker is crucial. It has to work as a business, and it has to work for you. Fulfillment and enjoyment go hand in hand. If you don't enjoy what you are doing, it is not going to fulfill you. The opposite is also true; if you enjoy what you are doing, you will feel some degree of fulfillment.

That is why you have to be introspective and 100 percent honest with yourself. It may sound good, but is it really good for you? I had to learn this lesson. I had to admit to myself a business just wasn't for me. I used to own a clothing store. At the time, it seemed like a good thing. It was in a local popular area, and I like clothes, so I thought, *Cool, I'll do this*. The way it works is you don't actually purchase the clothes in your store. You open up various credit accounts to stock your inventory and then you have a negotiated number of days to sell the items. So yes, I went to all the fashion shows, was able to pick out the clothes, and it was fun. But once I got into the business of knowing what it takes to operate and fund that store ... not so much. I realized it was more of a hobby for me, so I decided to close the store.

Now in my case, the clothing store didn't work for me. That doesn't mean it wouldn't work for someone else. I always tell people to not be discouraged while trying to find the business that works for them. It may take a few tries before you find the right fit. It also helps to do your due diligence before starting a business. If I had done more research, I probably would not have started the clothing store, but the lesson learned was far more important than the result of having had the store.

Once you find your passion, learn as much as you can

about that industry. Do enough research to ensure you have accurate information to determine if it will work for you. It is normal to be nervous or even fearful at the prospect of starting a business. Don't let the process of starting a business stop you. The knowledge you have collected is power. Once you have the information, it's time to hit the go button and do it.

When I was much younger, I didn't want to take the time to do my due diligence. I was the one saying, "I'm just going to do it." Was that the best method to use when going into business? No, it was not. But I was young, without a lot of responsibilities, so it was easier for me to just jump in. But as you get older, you don't want to just take a 50/50 chance on being in the right business. You don't want to just throw some money out there and start without having a game plan. That is a waste of precious time and resources. Do the research, get the information you need, and go from there. And listen, there's going to be some fear, but fear is not meant to stop you. It just wakes you up and keeps you sharp and focused.

I knew when the time came that my original franchise was no longer working for me because I learned to pay attention. So after several years, I could dissolve my contract. Today, I am working to establish my own franchise and making the business work for me.

The first step is to create the brand, which are the services you plan to offer and the method you will use to provide them. When you buy a franchise, all you are paying for are the brand and the franchisor's systems of operation. I am currently creating a brand. I have to create enough energy and positive influence around my brand to encourage other people to want to buy into my brand.

If you take H&R Block, Jackson Hewitt, or any other company out there in the tax industry, that's what they have done. They've put so much money into branding that when someone thinks of accounting firms, those are the first names that come to mind. Well, in my area, I'm working so they will think of my company when they need accounting and financial services.

Now while my business may lend itself to franchising, that won't be true of all businesses. I've researched a lot of franchises, and some of them just won't make sense. Franchising isn't a fit for every entrepreneur or every business. Some people start out with very big dreams. They think, *I'm going to have this local business and then I'll be everywhere in the country.* Just like that. Today, you are in your town; tomorrow, all fifty states. But there has to be a sense of realism when scaling what your business can do. Be realistic as you determine what model will work best for you to get there. You can be everywhere, but what is your growth plan for getting there?

When I was in graduate school, we had to research franchises and business models. I learned that Chick-fil-A does not offer franchising opportunities. They have an owner-operator model. I'm not saying one is better than the other, but some businesses are able to grow with franchises and others with an owner-operator model. I have considered a model where I own the real estate, the building, and the company but bring people in to manage different locations as owner-operators. That kind of expansion takes a certain personality and ability. This model would be ideal for someone who doesn't want to take risk or maybe doesn't have the necessary startup capital for traditional franchising.

If you want your business to grow as a franchise, you also need a system for quality control. A product purchased from a store in California should be consistent with a product purchased from a store in Illinois. Whatever model you choose, if you want a scalable business model, then every step along the way, an entrepreneur must decide whether it works for them.

If you want complete control over your brand, expanding with owner-operators may be the right choice for you. The built-in quality control of franchising may be a favorable option, as well. Whatever model you choose, you must constantly ask, "Is this the right choice for me?"

You also have to be aware of how fast you are growing. The business world is filled with cautionary tales of companies that took off, expanded too quickly, and then went bankrupt because they couldn't fulfill the demand. People become overzealous and think, *Oh, we can open stores everywhere.* So while we want success, we have to be aware of the negative effect growing too fast will have on your brand.

Starting a business is, of course, about making enough money to be sustainable. But money isn't the only deciding factor. Does the business work for you? Does it help fulfill your purpose? Being in business is also about learning and adapting.

Everyone works to get things—money, houses, cars, vacations, prestige, respect. But things come, and they go. Things rust, they fall apart, and they no longer work. At the end of the day, the knowledge you gain from going out and trying new things, no one can take that from you. You have to understand what works for you today, and you have the right to decide if it doesn't work for you tomorrow.

We are ever-evolving creatures; we are always changing. Business changes; the world changes. The only constant in life is change. So business has to continually work for you as you evolve. In retrospect, I have figured out that some of the deals I made when I was younger may not have been the best decisions. But at that time, they were great deals because I was just in the business of being in business. That's all that mattered. I just wanted to be in business!

But as I matured and started to understand my purpose-filled life, integrity became most important to me. Today I don't compromise my integrity for a deal, a person, or a contract—nothing! At the end of the day, I only get one me. I've built my reputation over a lifetime, but it can take mere minutes to tear it down. So I am careful not to compromise my integrity or reputation for any reason.

Now that I'm growing into the person I'm supposed to be spiritually, mentally, physically, and emotionally, I have to continually ask myself, "Does this deal work for me?" I have to be honest with myself. If the answer is no, I ask myself what it would take for me not to be in that business anymore. Even if it cost me money, I consider it some of the best education possible.

That is why I always say that the best education I've gotten I paid for. You aren't only educated in a classroom. Education comes from interaction and in the lessons we learn every day. Does your business work for you? Everyone has to answer that question professionally and personally. If it doesn't work for you, there is no point in putting the work into it. Find what does work for you and then it will be worth the sacrifices needed to make it a success.

CHAPTER 8
Use Someone Else's Money

In the neighborhood where I grew up, there were many small business owners. Go four or five blocks over, and you had drug dealers. Both enterprises were fueled by money. I was able to see at a very young age how drug dealers made all this money. Then I would look at my father, who was making less money than they were, but he was able to do so much more.

I remember thinking, *Okay, something doesn't add up here. Just having some money doesn't ultimately mean you can do the things you want to do. How does money work?* Even as a child, I wanted to know how money works. That has been my thing, and it led me down this path. My true passion is finance.

I wanted to major in finance, but I already had enough credits for my accounting degree. So instead of extending my time as an undergrad, I graduated with the accounting degree. I went to graduate school to get my MBA, where I could focus more on finance. It was always about learning how money works and understanding its function in our lives. My interest wasn't based on greed. Trust me; I have seen people who have a lot of money, and they are so unhappy. My dad was making money in a legitimate, honest way, and I would think, *He doesn't have as much as these other people I see making fast money illegally, but he's happier than all of them.* He didn't have to worry about going to jail, either. I knew a lot of other kids who went for the quick fix, the flashy car, expensive shoes. But I always wanted to earn and spend my money without sorrow.

One of the most important things to learn about finance is the value of using other people's money by obtaining loans, venture capital, or investors. This all goes back to chapter 2, where we establish a business versus a hustle. I am all for securing financing because it helps to grow your business much faster. You aren't trapped in a cash-only business, and you have resources to purchase inventory, build structures, and obtain property and whatever else you need to propel you to the next level.

Many people talk about debt as if it's taboo. You often hear people swear they won't take on debt. In reality, there's good debt and bad debt. We know what bad debt is. An example would be purchasing a house you cannot afford to pay for. It is taking an extravagant vacation and putting it all on credit cards you then must pay minimums on. It is spending sprees on new clothes and shoes you don't need and can't afford to pay for in cash.

But financing property or purchasing a structure for your business are examples of good debt. There is nothing wrong with good debt. The truth is there are tax write-offs for the good debt that you accumulate. More than that, if you owe someone money, it gives you the opportunity to be accountable and to establish a positive history of paying your debt. If you show you are responsible with money and debt, it indicates good character. Just the same, it will stain you forever if you become known as a shady businessperson. Build a reputation of being a responsible, accountable person, and that will follow you forever.

So you do not have to be fearful of debt. You often might find it hard to grow your business based on your current earnings, but seizing an opportunity to acquire good debt can increase your earning potential and elevate your business to the next level. If you ask almost any successful businessperson, you'll find they are not afraid to use someone else's money to expand their companies. If the terms aren't to their liking, they renegotiate the debt.

There is nothing wrong with using someone else's money if you have a business and not a hustle. You cannot use someone else's money if you have a hustle. You must be ready to get up, and get it done. That alone provides a building block toward structure.

If you are anything like me, you won't enjoy owing money to anyone. However, sometimes it is necessary. I can remember when my dad's waste management company only had one truck. I saw an opportunity to take on massive amounts of business because another waste management company went out of business. The company that was folding wanted me to take on their clients, but I was unable to seize the opportunity with just one truck. So I went to the bank and explained what I wanted to do. I told them about my business, how long I had been in business, its profits, how many clients I had—all to show the bank that I had a legitimate business. Then I told them about the opportunity I had to bring on multiple clients if I could get the equipment I needed to handle the volume. The bank looked at my business plan and approved a loan to purchase the equipment and everything else I needed to service the new clients.

The lesson here is that I was not afraid to use someone else's money when it was necessary. I wasn't afraid to be accountable to the bank for the loan because it allowed me to seize an opportunity. This is also an example of the importance of asking the right question. The right question was, Can I get a loan? I asked the question, they said yes, and I could propel my business further than where my business alone could have gone.

However, even with good debt, be careful not to overextend yourself. For example, mortgages are considered good debt partly because you build equity, and they have incredible tax benefits. At the same time, like we witnessed during the housing crises in 2008, even good debt can lead to bad situations. In the years leading up to the recession, many people took out loans that offered extremely low interests rates for the first few years and then the interest rates went up. People couldn't afford their increased mortgages, foreclosures became rampant, and the housing market crashed along with the overall economy.

Most people blamed the lenders, saying they were at fault. But my philosophy is a little bit different. If I'm paying $600 in rent and just getting by but purchase a home because someone says I can buy a house for just an additional $250 a month, I am being irresponsible. And to be honest, you can't own a home for just $850 a month because a whole lot of other expenses come with owing a home.

The lesson here is there is no "pie in the sky." If a deal seems too good to be true, it almost certainly is. Don't let people take advantage of you. Know your purpose. You've got to be really clear about where you currently are in your business and your finances. You need to be accountable. You need a business, not a hustle. And you need the right business structure and setup.

Everything we've talked about so far is the foundation for financing your business. Going to a bank is probably the first kind of financing people think of. But there are also partnership opportunities that may work for your business. Some people look at getting a partner as a last-resort strategy. But in my experience, sometimes it's great to bring on a partner because he or she may have a separate set of skills that can be beneficial to the company. The personality of the business owner dictates whether a partnership will work. You have to be honest with yourself. Are you willing to part with something that you've built to take it to the next level?

A great example of something like that is the TV series *Shark Tank*. People come on there with great ideas, or they've built prototypes of products. They come on the show and say, "Now I want to take this to the next level. I want to get into the stores. I want to mass produce this product." In order to accomplish these things, they need capital; they need money. At some point, all entrepreneurs have to decide if they want to be a mom-and-pop business or to grow?

For as many positives as there are in a partnership, there can be drawbacks. While I'm currently a sole proprietor, I had a partnership with the very first business I started. That partnership didn't work out well and left a bad taste in my mouth for other partnerships. If I were to ever do another partnership, I would consider someone I have a mutual respect for rather than someone I only have a friendship with. I had to learn the hard way that sometimes partnering with friends gets messy.

When friends become business partners, it can be difficult to leave the friendship at the door and remember that you are running a business. When you deal with friends, you need to establish professional boundaries early on. Because someone is a friend, you sometimes don't take the time to clearly define the duties and responsibilities expected from each other to help prevent resentments later. When a business associate doesn't carry his or her weight, it upsets you. But when a friend doesn't do his or her part, you feel betrayed. It can get ugly fast.

When you partner with strangers, you have no expectations other than getting the business done. Friends may think otherwise, creating conversations like, "What? You mean I actually have to come in on Fridays? You know I like playing golf on Friday." "Well, yeah, but I need the inventory done on Friday."

So it's more likely you'll run into problems with friends and family than when you partner with just business associates. A prime example is my own father. When I was younger, I worked for his company. Working for family can be a special challenge because there's no such thing as off-time. You could be home at 8:00 at night, and if something needs to get done, they want it done now instead of tomorrow, during your regular work hours. I remember telling my dad, "This is business over here; this is family over here." But to him, there was no line to be drawn.

There was also the matter of pay. I would work a full week and expect to get my full paycheck. But then I'd look at the check and ask, "What is this?" My father would answer, "Well, you live in my house, you eat my food …" But it's your dad, so what are you going to do? Quit? That's why I say working for family and with friends can be difficult.

That complicated dynamic also comes up if family or friends invest in your business. It's one thing if you go to a venture capitalist, and your business doesn't work out. Assuming risk is what they do. They understand there is always a chance a business won't succeed. The same is true with banks, which is why it can be so hard to get a loan. But if it fails, a loan officer or venture capitalist doesn't think any less of you or think you've betrayed them in any way. They write it off, they go on, life continues. But with a family member or friend, the fallout can be immense. So while I encourage you to use someone else's money, be very careful about whose money you choose to use.

When I had a partner, I was young and so eager to be in business. I thought, *Okay, yeah. I want to do this. Let's do it.* He had the cash I needed, so we partnered up. I eventually came to realize this guy had the worst spending habits of anybody I'd ever known. When you're partners with someone, whatever they go out and do in the company name, guess what? You become liable for it. Even though you didn't actually do it—like run up debt—in the eyes of the law, you did. I'll just say it: My partner and I ended on bad terms. So when that happened I said, "Okay! I am done with that." There was a clause in the contract that basically said if either of us defaulted on our obligations, the contract became null and void. So I ended up getting out of that contract with my partner by working with the franchise owners and signed my own solo contract.

The ways things are for me now, I don't necessarily need an equity partner. I need more of a sweat equity partner. I need someone who is able to work just as hard, or even harder, than I do. You'll find that's a typical evolution in business. Your needs starting out are usually financial. Once you have been in business for a while, and the business is established, your financial needs change.

Everything in finance goes back to accountability. You need to know whether you need a partner or just an investor, and you need to know the difference between the two. You always have to watch your spending habit and your growth plan. I mean, you don't have to be the biggest right out of the box. Get into the business, get it going, and keep it going until you have the opportunity to expand. Through it all, restraint, patience, responsibility, and using other people's money are the keys to maintaining a financially sound business.

CHAPTER 9

Start the Way You Want to Finish

We all run the race with the finish line in mind. But in business, there is no finish line as long as your company is up and running. Business owners must have the foresight to make decisions today that can keep businesses growing, succeeding, and pushing their owners past the point others set as their finish lines.

You hear about glass ceilings and barriers that can hold you back, and they do exist—if you let them. There is nothing holding you back from pursuing your vision if you are determined enough, so start the way you want to finish. Think about where you are today, envision yourself ten years down the line, and ask yourself where you want to be in a decade. You should always work today with the future in mind. Keeping that vision out front will help you make better long-term decisions for the business.

Once you have the vision, you have to stay in the vision. I am talking about my spirituality. God will not give you the vision without giving you the tools to get there. You don't have to be perfect because you have everything you need already. You have the vision. You only have to get up, and go get it. Sometimes we have to get out of our own way and trust that we have everything we need, even when we have to ask for help.

In the game Monopoly, there are get out of jail free cards, but in real life, there are no such passes. So stay away from going to jail, and keep your nose clean. If it sounds too good to be true, it probably isn't true. The more you go and grow, you will be presented with things that are not good for you. But keep that vision in mind to start the way you want to finish. Understand that the decisions you make today impact your destiny. Remind yourself every day that you are starting the way you want to finish.

Right now, it may just be a sno-cone stand on the corner, but it could develop into the next Ben & Jerry's. Envision it! You must think like you are already the king or queen of ice even when you're a local street vendor. It is all in the vision of your destiny. Don't think in terms of small fish, big pond. You almost must have blinders on because as long as you are doing your best and producing the best product, you can't compare yourself to others or feel discouraged because somebody else might be bigger or doing better. That's just a distraction. If you keep your vision and do what you're supposed to, your time will come.

That said, you also have to be comfortable with understanding that you may never see the finish line, but your children's children will. Generational blessings ... finish it!

After seeing so many businesses over the years and after having my own business for years, I think this is one of the most important lessons to learn if you want to start a business. How you start is how you will finish. If you start with integrity, you are likely to finish with integrity. If you start with selling shoddy products or offering bad customer service, you'll finish a failure.

My dad would always say you have to do it right from the start because, "You can't always go back and try to correct what is wrong." I see it all the time; trying to correct bad behavior is the hardest thing in the world. It is almost easier to get new employees than it is to correct a staff who has no regard for customer service, no pride in their work, or no commitment to your business.

When you have a business, every day is a new start. The marketplace is always changing; your business is always evolving. You have to always evaluate and adjust your long-term plans. The fundamentals—dedication, trust, attention to detail, good service, a commitment to quality—will always count. If you let those fundamentals slide, your business will suffer.

Starting how you want to finish also means having an exit strategy in place, preferably before you even start the business. Yes, your exit plans may change as the years go by, but you should still have considered whether you are planning to build a business and then sell it after ten years or so to start a new company—a pattern adopted by many serial entrepreneurs. You may want to start a business that you envision passing down for generations in your family. Whatever your vision, an exit strategy helps you keep your eye on the future and make decisions accordingly.

Keeping an eye on the end and developing an exit strategy goes hand in hand with starting the way you want to finish. My personal plan right now is to be in business until I'm around fifty-five years old. By that time, I think I may not want to deal with all the ups and downs of being in business anymore. After I get out of business, I want to be a professor. That vision informs the decisions I make today.

There are also people who envision a different kind of serial entrepreneurialism. Instead of selling a business once it's up and running, they want to maintain ownership as they go off to start a new, unrelated business. While there are some very famous examples of people who have done that, it's hard to do. It is difficult practically and emotionally. Besides, there are only so many hours in a day. In my experience, it's hard to be so deeply rooted or invested in something and then just walk away from it and have no further input in its operations. Like with my company, once I grow it to a certain place, I cannot imagine just handing it over to someone and saying, "Okay, I'll still own it, but you run it. I'm not going to have any more input. I'm going to go do something else and watch you run it from afar." I don't think that is possible from a true entrepreneurial standpoint. You are either all in, or you cut the cord, move on, and don't look back.

There are businesspeople who acquire companies that other people have built and end up owning a dozen companies. That's a different type of entrepreneur. They didn't think of the business, create it, build it, sacrifice for it, and bring it to fruition. They just buy up profitable companies that exist because of other people's visions. They specialize in acquisitions.

One way entrepreneurs expand without selling is to expand vertically because that kind of growth is still based on the core business. For example, like when I expanded my accounting business by offering annuities and other investments. It is all still based on money and finance. Or say I have a restaurant I want to franchise. Well, I might get into buying a small hotel. Both are part of the service and hospitality industry, and hotels need restaurants, so I can put my restaurant in my new hotel. From there, I might start a catering company. That is vertical growth and a fundamental foundation of entrepreneurial growth.

There is strength in vertical integration. If the restaurant business goes through a slump, your other businesses can make up for it. Peaks and valleys are part of business, and diversifying helps protect you during the slow times. Let's think for a second about Microsoft. Bill Gates was simply offering a computer operating system. Then he moved into word-processing programs and then business software and publishing software. Then came hardware and smartphones. All are tied together by Microsoft's ever-evolving operating system. Make sure you don't stretch yourself thin on something that's totally unrelated. Instead, diversify within your core business. Look from within first, because if this is what you're already vested in and where you believe you can make impactful change and fulfill your purpose, look for new business ventures or ideas that are related.

More than anything, I want you to be inspired after reading this book. I have the same hope for my face-to-face clients. After all the conversations, after working together for weeks, after all is said and done, I want you to not just believe you can do it but to *know* you can do it. Once we've finished developing a plan and putting it to paper, it's time to execute. I check in with my clients after six months or maybe a year. The follow-up is very important to me because people often need encouragement, support, or sometimes just to vent to someone who knows what they are going through. It's rejuvenating; it gives them a second wind and helps them to keep going. So don't be hesitant to reach out to positive, encouraging people who will help you realize, "Okay, I got it. I'm going to keep going."

If you've stayed with me to the end of this book, I want

you to have so much confidence that you're saying, "Hey, I can do this," not, "Well, I'm thinking about it." I want you to know in your heart that you are going to get it done. I want you to be so ready that you decide, "I cannot wait. Life is too short, so I am going to start today."

I want you to be all in.

I want you to be accountable to yourself, your idea, and to God.

I want you to fulfill your purpose.

I want you to be confident to ask the right questions.

I want you to make your business work for you.

I want you to use other people's money to reach your goals.

I want you to get down to business.

www.ingramcontent.com/pod-product-compliance
Lightning Source LLC
Chambersburg PA
CBHW030856180526
45163CB00004B/1594